Joseph Jastrow

The Time-Relations of Mental Phenomena

Joseph Jastrow

The Time-Relations of Mental Phenomena

ISBN/EAN: 9783743394032

Manufactured in Europe, USA, Canada, Australia, Japa

Cover: Foto ©Thomas Meinert / pixelio.de

Manufactured and distributed by brebook publishing software
(www.brebook.com)

Joseph Jastrow

The Time-Relations of Mental Phenomena

THE TIME-RELATIONS OF MENTAL PHENOMENA.

THE study of the time relations of mental phenomena is important from several points of view: it serves as an index of mental complexity, giving the sanction of objective demonstration to the results of subjective observation; it indicates a mode of analysis of the simpler mental acts, as well as the relation of these laboratory products to the processes of daily life; it demonstrates the close inter-relation of psychological with physiological facts, an analysis of the former being indispensable to the right comprehension of the latter; it suggests means of lightening and shortening mental operations, and thus offers a mode of improving educational methods; and it promises in various directions to deepen and widen our knowledge of those processes by the complication and elaboration of which our mental life is so wonderfully built up. It is only within very recent years that this department of research has been cultivated; and it is natural that the results of different workers, involving variations in method and design, should show points of difference. In spite of these it seems possible to present a systematic sketch of what has been done, with due reference to the ultimate goal as well as to the many gaps still to be filled. It is with the object of furnishing such a general view that the following exposition has been attempted.

Rate of Nervous Impulses.

While it follows, as a very natural consequence of the modern view of the relation between body and mind, that mental processes, however simple, should occupy time, it must be remembered that the very opposite opinion has been held by serious thinkers. It has been argued as a proof of the immateriality of thought that its operations were out of relation to time, and the expression "quick as thought" has come to indicate a maximum of speed. It being established that so comparatively simple a process as sensation involves the passage of an impulse along nerve-fibres, it is plain that the rate of travelling of this impulse sets a limit to the time of the entire process, as well as of all more complicated mental operations in which sensations are involved. The physiologist Johannes Müller, writing in 1844, despaired of our ever being able to measure the time of so excessively rapid and short a movement; but before the close of the same decade, Helmholtz measured the rate in the nerve of the frog, finding it to be about 86 feet per second. Though somewhat greater in man. 110 feet per second, this movement is extremely slow compared with the velocity of light or even sound: indeed, it is only slightly faster than the fastest express train.

Müller writes: " We shall probably never secure the means of ascertaining the speed of nerve activity, because we lack the comparison of enormous distances from which the speed of a movement, in this respect analogous to light, could be calculated;" and again: "The time in which a sensation proceeds from the periphery to the brain and the spinal cord, and is followed by a re-action at the periphery by means of muscular contractions, is infinitely small and immeasurable." It is interesting to note how very crude were the conceptions of the older physiologists upon this point. Haller (1762) tells us of one who, following the view that the nervous impulse was a fluid, and its action analagous to that of the blood, found the "nerve tubes" of the heart to be 2,880 million times as narrow as the aorta, and concluded that the nervous impulse travelled proportionately faster than the blood, thus making its rate 57,600 million feet per second. Haller himself measured the maximum rapidity of short rhythmical movements, and (falsely), assuming that the impulse travelled to and from muscle and brain between each contraction, found an (accidentally not very erroneous) speed of 9,000 feet per second. The method introduced by Helmholtz, and improved by himself and others, consists in excising a muscle with a long stretch of nerve attached, and connecting the muscle with a lever, so that every contraction of it is registered upon the quickly moving surface of a revolving drum or a swinging pendulum. By electrically stimulating the nerve first at a point near to and then at a point far off from the muscle, two curves are recorded, the latter of which is found to leave the base line a trifle after the former. A tuning-fork writes its vibrations beneath these records, and enables us to measure how much later the second contraction began, while the distance travelled in this time is that between the two points of stimulation on the nerve. It has been attempted to measure this rate in man by having the subject re-act once to a stimulus applied to the foot, and again to a stimulus at the hip, or some point nearer the spinal cord, and counting the difference in time as due to the difference in length of nerve traversed. While the method is necessarily inaccurate, and other factors contribute to the difference in time, the majority of the determinations indicate a rate of between 30 and 40 metres (100 to 130 feet) per second. These determinations apply to sensory nerves: for the motor nerves of man, Helmholtz has found, by a method closely similar to that employed upon the frog, a rate of 110 feet per second. The most influential of the conditions affecting this rate is temperature: cold decreases and heat increases it, the extremes of variation being 30 to 90 metres. Under normal conditions it seems fair to regard the rate for both motor and sensory nerves of man as about 110 feet per second.

Analysis of Re-actions.

A great variety of actions may be viewed as responses to stimuli. There is a flash of light, and we wink; a burning cinder falls upon the hand, and we draw it away; a bell rings, and the engineer starts his train, or the servant opens the door, or we go down to dinner; the clock strikes, and we stop work, or go to meet an appointment. Again, in such an occupation as copying, every letter or word seen acts as a stimulus, to which the written letter or word is the response; in piano playing, and the guidance of complicated machinery, we see more elaborate instances of similar processes. The printer distributing "pi," the post-office clerk sorting the mails, are illustrations of quick forms of re-action, in which the different letters of the alphabet or the different addresses of the mail matter act as the stimuli, and the placing them in their appropriate places follows as the response. In many games, such as tennis or cricket, the various ways in which the ball is seen to come to the striker are the stimuli, for each variation of which there is a precise and complex form of response in the mode of returning the ball. In military drill the various words of command are the stimuli, and the actions thus induced the responses; and such illustrations could be multiplied indefinitely. In all these actions the time-relations are more or less definite and important, but a useful study of them presupposes a careful and systematic analysis of the processes therein involved. We recognize that certain of the above actions are more complicated than others, and we must inquire in what this complication consists. In the process as usually presented the nature of the re-action depends upon the nature of the stimulus, a variation in the one being concomitant with a variation in the other. The piano player, seeing a certain mark on the page, strikes a certain key on the key-board, but strikes a different key if this mark be differently placed; the soldier varies his movement according to the word of command, and so on with most of the others. All such actions involve at least three processes: (1) the recognition of the sense impression, (2) the performance of the appropriate action, and (3) the association of the one with the other. The recognition involves the appreciation of the *presence* together with the appreciation of the *nature* of the sense-impression; and the movement involves the contraction of muscles together with the initiation of the impulse. We obtain the simplest form of re-action by limiting the stimulus to a single definite one, and having one and the same response irrespective of the nature of the stimulus. The subject expects the stimulus the nature of which he knows, and is ready to signal, by a simple movement agreed upon in advance, *merely* that the impression has been received. This we shall speak of as a "simple re-action." It occurs whenever a certain sense-impression is agreed upon as a signal for the execution of a simple movement. The time-keeper pressing the spring of the stop-watch, or the racer starting off as soon as the pistol is fired or the word is given, are instances of simple re-actions. It should be noted that the simplicity of the act refers primarily to the subject's fore-knowledge of what is to occur; the nature of the sense-impression, as of the motion, is known in advance, the association between the two being in the main artificial. Inasmuch as the more elaborate mental processes involve those of the simple re-action, our first step must be to determine its elements and their time-relations.

The Elements of a Simple Re-action.

The several elements of a simple re-action have been variously analyzed by different observers, but all recognize the *physiological* and the specially *psychological* portions of the process. The physiological time-elements include, (*a*) the time for the sense-organ to respond to an impression, i.e., to overcome its inertia; (*b*) the time for the passage of the impulse inward along nerves (and spinal cord), with the various delays whenever the impulse enters or passes through cells; (c) the return passage of the motor impulse from the brain to (spinal chord and) nerve and muscle; and (d) the time for the contraction of the muscle. The time thus left unaccounted for is that taken up by the psychological process, the transformation of the sensory into the motor impulse,—a process taking place in the brain, but as to the precise nature of which we have no definite information. The separate determination of each of the physiological factors enables us to find approximately the duration of the central process. As a sufficiently typical case we may accept the estimate of Cattell, that, in re-acting to a light by pressing the key with the finger, the time needed by the impulse to travel from eye to brain and from brain to spinal cord and finger is about 50σ;[1] the latent time in the muscle, during which it overcomes its inertia, is judged from experiments upon the frog to be about 5σ to 10σ; and experiment gives a value of 15σ to 20σ for stimulating the retina and initiating the impulse. As the entire re-action occupied about 150σ we conclude that in this case the physiological and the psychological portions of the process occupy about equal times. One may obtain a fair notion of the rate of these processes by the following simple experiment. A score or so of persons form a chain by joining hands, and at a given signal a certain member of the group sharply presses the hand of his neighbor, who in turn imparts the pressure as quickly as possible to *his* neighbor, and so on until the impression has gone the rounds. An outsider keeps the time (which may be done with sufficient accuracy by counting the ticks of a watch, usually fifths of a second) from the moment of giving the signal to start to the moment of receiving the signal from the last member of the group that the impression has been circulated. The entire time divided by the number of persons in the group (or better, by that

---

[1] The sign σ indicates one one-thousandth of a second.

number plus two to include the re-actions at starting and stopping) gives an average simple re-action time, which, though long at first, is reduced after a little practice to a sixth or a seventh of a second.   On this basis one may calculate that if a number of men, stretching out their arms and grasping one another's hands, were stationed in a straight line, it would take three minutes to send a message in the manner just described along a mile of this human telegraph.

(a) The inertia of sense-organs has been variously determined.   One method measures how closely impressions may follow one another without fusing.   The time thus measured is the minimum time during which the sense-organ may be stimulated and recover sufficiently to receive a second stimulation.   This process thus includes something more than the one we desire to measure, and may perhaps be regarded as furnishing a maximum time of the sensory inertia.   Here again various circumstances influence the determinations, the chief ones being the sense-organ in question and the clearness and intensity of the impression.   Sectors of black and white upon a disc revolving in daylight at the rate of about 25 times a second fuse into a uniform gray, making the inertia of the retina under these conditions about 40σ. In weak light (moonlight) the time lengthens to about 100σ. The same experiment has been made with sectors of different colors, with the disc stationary and the light reflected from a rotating mirror, with a vibrating point of light; and, while all these variations somewhat affect the result, the majority of the determinations indicate a fusion at 30 to 40 impressions a second, or a duration of 33σ to 25σ.   For sound, different observers have chosen different points for measurement. The slowest rate of impressions fusing into a musical sound has been fixed at between 30 and 40 per second; but Helmholtz has shown that the interference of sound-waves perceptible as beats does not escape detection when recurring as rapidly as 132 per second.   For non-musical sounds, such as electric clicks, a still higher rate has been found.   In touch we distinguish differences of feeling when impressions are rapid enough to fuse but not rapid enough to fuse perfectly.   The smoothness of a polished surface is not obtained until the impressions occur 480 to 640 times a second (Valentin).   For taste and smell the period, though not accurately determined, is undoubtedly very long. Here the time needed to reach the somewhat concealed sense-organs is considerable, and the chemical processes involved are relatively slow in action. The influence of the mode of activity of the sense-organ upon its period of stimulation is further illustrated in the long inertia period of the probably chemical action of vision compared with the short period of the mechanical senses of hearing and touch. This view is also supported by the fact that the period for the retina is shortened if the eye be directly stimulated electrically. Another mode of experimenting consists in applying a stimulus for the minimum time during which it can be recognized. The time thus measured will be shorter than the other, for it tells us only how long is needed for initiating the process of recognition sufficiently to have it continue to completion (probably after the stimulus ceases). This is indeed a surprisingly short time. Cattell and Sanford independently found that a color or a letter could be recognized when visible for only from 1σ to 5σ, while less recently Baxt recognized 6 to 7 letters when exposed for only 5σ. Others have calculated that the maximum effect of an impression is not reached until from 50σ to 150σ, but these determinations seem to involve some mental process of recognition. Whether or not some such process of recognition is involved is not quite clear. Unless specially prevented, the recognition will take place on the basis of the after-image, a few thousandths of a second being sufficient to initiate the process. By following the impression by a strong flash of light, and thus nullifying the after-image, Baxt found a longer time needed to recognize a more complicated impression. Within 10σ to 15σ, one letter; within 24σ, three letters; within 34σ, four letters, could be recognized. This only partially excludes the effect of the after-image, so that perhaps the results with complicated impressions are minimum "recognition times," and those with simple impressions "inertia times." Another method, that of Exner, is similar to the method of fusion. It consists in finding how closely two impressions, stimulating slightly different portions of the sense-organ, may follow one another and yet be recognized as successive. Optical impressions were so recognized when falling at an interval of 44σ on two points of the retina near the centre .011 millimetres apart, a longer time being necessary if the points are away from the centre of the retina. It seems probable that this process is more complicated than the one we are attempting to study. While the data thus at our disposal do not allow us to fix accurately the time of sensory inertia, the estimate provisionally accepted in the text cannot be far from the truth, being rather over than under estimated. The methods of measuring the rate of nervous impulses (b) and (c) have already been described. The inertia of the muscle and the time of its contraction are determined upon the same apparatus by observing how much after the shock is given the curve leaves the base-line.

Reflex, Automatic, and Voluntary Re-actions.

The term "re-action" as here used is not intended to include all responses to stimuli. The above instanced forms of re actions present various grades of naturalness, utility, and habituation; that is, the association between motion and stimulus has by practice become more or less close and easy. Copying, for example, may become so entirely automatic that it runs on of itself without the need of renewed volitional effort. The actions recognized as reflex take place in spite of all volition. The re-actions here considered are limited to those requiring some degree of voluntary effort for their execution, though this may be almost indefinitely reduced by practice. The reflex act takes very much less time for its execution than the voluntary: the time for winking has been determined by Exner to be something over 50σ. In other words, it takes about three times as long to signal by a voluntary closure of the eye-lid that an impression has been received as to perform the same act reflexly when the eye is threatened. The utility of this quick action for the protection of the eye is evident; and other useful re-actions, such as those of flight and escape in timid animals, seem to be of a similar nature. The quick movements of defence when attacked, of regaining one's balance when slipping, are so immediately useful and so well inculcated in the organism as often to surprise us by their quickness. Most of these actions can also be performed voluntarily, but neither so well nor so quickly; it is therefore difficult to subject them to experiment. As already indicated, in the ordinary re-action there is little naturalness in the connection of stimulus and movement, the same type of movement being used for all. The experienced re-actor becomes accustomed to signal by the finger movement that the operation required of him has been accomplished, but hardly associates this movement with any particular stimulus.

It is perhaps well to add that the great saving of time in actions that have become automatic (such as is seen in the experienced piano player or post-office clerk as compared with the beginner), is in great part due to the increased facility of doing several things at once and not serially, a factor that enters only in a small degree into the simple re-action. The processes we should be most interested in measuring are those most closely approaching the operations of daily thought, so that the inference from experiment to practice shall be as direct as possible. This, however, it is difficult to do, because every-day mental processes do not present the simplicity of conditions required by experiment. Accordingly the method has been to study the simplest re-actions, and then take into account the circumstances in which our usual mental operations differ from them.

Conditions Affecting Simple Re-action Times.

Referring to the accompanying tab'e for a general view of the time-relations of simple re-actions, we may pass at once to the topic of greatest interest, viz., the influences by which they are quickened or retarded. These may be considered as (A) objective, or affecting the conditions of the experiment, and (B) subjective, affecting the attitude of the re-actor.

$(A, 1)$ *The Nature of the Impression.* The distinctive characteristics of a simple re-action being in the attitude of the re-actor, it would seem that its time could be little affected by the nature of the impression. The motor signalling process is the same, the connection between the im-

Table of Simple Re-action Times.

No.	Nature of Sense-Impression.	Nature of Re-action.	Observer.	Time.	Remarks.
I	Visual (various kinds)	Finger.	Average of many	185	
II	Tactile "	"	"	145	Average of all parts of body.
III	Auditory "	"	"	139	
IV	Temperature (cold)	"	Steinbach	161	
V	" (warm)	"	"	177	
VI	Light of Intensity I	"	Berger & Cattell } Av.	210	The intensity in terms of a common unit were as I, 29, 123, 315, 1000, the two highest intensities not being determinable.
VII	" II	"	"	184	
VIII	" III	"	"	174	
IX	" IV	"	"	170	
X	" V	"	"	163	
XI	" VI	"	"	156	
XII	" VII	"	"	148	
XIII	Touch (electric shock)	"	Exner.	139	On the hand.
XIV	"	"	"	175	On the foot.
XV	Sound (low)	"	Wundt.	175	With preparatory signal.
XVI	"	"	"	266	Without " "
XVII	Sound	"	Berger & Cattell } Av.	124	Preparatory signal at regular intervals.
XVIII	"	"	"	165	Preparatory signal irregularly varied within 15 seconds.
XIX	Sound { Average of weak and loud sound.	"	Wundt.	121	Intensity of sound known.
XX	"	"	Münsterberg.	203	Intensity of sound unknown.
XXI	"	"	"	162	Attention directed to sensation.
XXII	Sound	"	"	120	Attention directed to movement.
XXIII	Touch (electric shock in forearm).	By opening and closing jaw. } Av. Orchansky.		155	Normal.
XXIV	"	"	"	105	8 minutes after taking 60 ccm. of rum.
XXV	"	"	"	225	30 " " " " "

pression and movement is about equally artificial in all cases, so that the chief variability must be in the time needed for receiving the impression. For the different senses this time is different. Taking the general average of all the observations accessible to me, I find, for hearing, 138σ; for touch, 148σ; for sight, 185σ. This order is quite constant with the different observers, the long time of visual re-actions being referable to the long inertia period of that sense, as well as to the small perceptive area of the retina, necessitating a precise accommodation, — a condition not always supplied in the above experiments. This view is strengthened by the shortening in the re-action time (by 36σ for Exner, by 24σ for v. Wittich) when the eye is stimulated electrically. In re-acting to a temperature sensation, care must be taken not to re-act to the sensation of contact with the skin. Where this has been done it has been found that the re-action to the sensations of temperature is longer than to contact, and that the re-action to heat is longer than to cold. Thus, Vintschgau and Steinach re-act to a pressure on various points of the head in 109σ, to a sensation of cold in 135σ, of heat in 146σ, similar values for various points of the hand being 121σ, 188σ, 209σ. The researches of Goldscheider agree with these in the main, but make the difference between the re action times to heat and to cold much greater. The senses of taste and smell clearly illustrate the effect of the kind of stimulation, for here the relative inaccessibility of the sense organs and the slowly acting chemical processes involved lead to a long re-action time. Though experimentation is difficult and uncertain in these senses, we may cite for smell the results of Moldenhauer on the odors of various oils, centring about 300σ (oil of roses 273σ, camphor 321σ, musk 319σ, ether 255σ, etc.), and for taste, of Hönigschmied, who re-acts to various tastes on the tip of the tongue in 182σ, though other subjects require about 300σ. On the back of the tongue the time is much longer, and it varies for different tastes, being longest for bitter, shortest for salt, and about equal for sweet and sour. Within the same sense the re-action time will vary according to the nature and place of the stimulus. The above cited differences for tastes and smells show this; and for different visual impressions, for different tones, for contact at different parts of the body, different results have been obtained, referable to slight variations in sensibility, length of nerve traversed, clearness of the impression, and the like. These minor differences are not easily established, but the following may be cited. Exner re-acts to an electric shock on the hand in 132σ, on the forehead in 137σ, on the foot in 175σ; v. Wittich re-acts to a point on the back of the finger in a longer time than to one on the front, 144σ and 156σ, and regards the difference as due to a difference of sensibility. Hall and Kries clearly show that the re-action to a point looked at in indirect vision is longer than to one in direct vision, 195σ and 235σ, and find further differences according as the point is above or below, inside or outside, the retinal centre. A high tone is re-acted to more quickly than a low one, and so on.

It is easier to demonstrate the influence of (2) *the intensity of the stimulus.* Within limits, intense stimuli affect sense-organs more quickly than weak ones, and, roughly speaking, an increase in the intensity of the stimulus is concomitant with a decrease in the re-action time. According to Wundt, the noise of a hammer falling respectively from heights of 1, 4, 8, and 16 millimetres was re-acted to in 217σ, 146σ, 132σ, and 135σ, and the sound of a ball falling from heights of 2, 5, 25, and 55 centimetres in 176σ, 161σ, 159σ, and 94σ respectively. Exner varied the length and therefore the brilliancy of an electric spark from 0.5 to 7 millimetres and obtained a steadily decreasing re-action time of 158σ to 123σ. More complete are the observations of Berger and Cattell, who found that as the light increased from

7 to 23, to 123, to 315, to 1.000, and to two greater but not determinable degrees of intensity (as compared with a small unit of light), the re-action times fell (average of two observers) from 210σ to 184σ, to 174σ, to 170σ, to 169σ, to 156σ, to 148σ. For sound, as the ball fell from heights of 60, 160, 300, and 560 millimetres the re-action times were 151σ, 146σ, 127σ, and 123σ. For electrical touch excitations, re-actions to four grades of stimuli separated by equally perceptible differences were made (average of two observers) in 173σ, 159σ, 145σ, and 145σ. Wundt regards the difference in re-action times of the different senses as in part referable to differences in intensity, and, when re-acting to just perceptible intensities of sensation in various senses, finds about the same long time for each, 330σ.

3. *The Mode of Re-action.* The various movements by which we may signal that a sensation has been received may differ in the ease of their execution, in the length of nerve traversed, as well as in the naturalness of association with the impression. Such differences, however, seem to be small; when once the movement is understood and anticipated, the difference in the times of its execution is slight. Thus, Münsterberg found, in testing the re-action of each of the five fingers, that while at first the thumb and little finger re-acted more slowly than the others, after some practice the times of all were substantially the same. Féré, however, has some results suggesting that the fingers making the strongest movements re-act in the shortest times. Very interesting, too, is the experiment of Ewald in which the stimulus, an electric shock, is given to the finger in the very key by which the re-action is signalled, the re-action consisting in the very natural movement of drawing the finger away. Under these circumstances he found a brief and constant time of 90σ. Both Vintschgau and Cattell have compared the time of re-acting by closing a key with the finger and by speaking a word, and find the vocal method

the longer by about 16σ and 30σ respectively. Differences in re-acting from the two sides of the body have been observed by some, the right side showing the shorter re-action, but this difference can hardly be considered as constant. Orchansky has shown in one case that the movements of inhibition take about the same time as those of excitation of a muscle, and it would be possible to study the relative ease of various movements by this method. A practical example is furnished by the commands of military drill, the words, "carry," "present," etc., announcing the mode of re-action for the performance of which the following word, "arms," is the signal.

(B) We pass next to the more important *subjective* factors, referring in the main to the *expectation* and the *attention*. While nothing has been definitely said upon this point, the implication has been that the subject tries his utmost to re-act as quickly as possible, and that he knows the nature of the experiment. While the influences now to be discussed seem to be general in their effect, making the nervous system at one time a better and again a worse re-acting apparatus, they may, in certain respects, be subjected to a more definite analysis. We begin with (1) *the subject's fore-knowledge of what is to take place.* We may anticipate the outcome of experimentation on this point by formulating the law that the more definite the fore-knowledge of the subject the quicker the re-action. Apparently there is a process that must be gone through with in each re-action, and the better prepared the subject is for this,—that is, the more of this process gone through with before the giving of the stimulus,—the less of it falls within the measured interval. The precise nature of this process is a difficult and much discussed problem. It may be sufficient to note at present that the re-action to a certain stimulus cannot but imply in some sense the distinction of that stimulus from the many others by which we are constantly surrounded. If the subject be re-acting to a visual impression, he will prob ably not press the key should a noise occur in the room or something accidentally come in contact with his hand. To re-act to a visual impression thus implies the distinction of that from other impressions. It implies the identification of the expected with the existing impression. Just as we recognize an appearance in the heavens or under the micro scope more readily when we know where and what to look for, or as we immediately recognize an almost forgotten ac quaintance when expecting him, though at a chance meeting we might have passed him without recognition, so we re-act to an impression most quickly when it is most definitely ex pected, with regard to its nature, its time, place of ap pearance, and the like. This expectation may be more or less specific, and an interesting series of experiments consists in varying the fore-knowledge of the subject while still leav ing it definite enough to call the result a simple re-action. (a) We may leave the precise *time* of the appearance of the stimulus undetermined. This may be done by experiment ing with and without a preparatory signal, preceding the stimulus by a regular interval. Wundt re-acted to the sound of a ball falling from a height of 25 centimetres in 76σ with a preparatory signal, but in 253σ if no such signal preceded; to a ball falling five centimetres, in 175σ in the first case, and 266σ in the second. Martius re-acts to the sound of a falling hammer in 127σ when preceded at a regular interval by a signal, but in 178σ without the signal. Dwelshauvers re-acts in 193σ in the former case, in 236σ in the latter (average of "sensory" and "motor" re-actions). The time between the signal and stimulus is here regular, and the most favora ble time seems to be about two seconds. Lange found the time with an interval of two seconds less than with one of one or three seconds. Dwelshauvers varied the interval from a second and a half to three, and then to six seconds, and finds the shortest re-actions at a second and a half. Martius has experimented with intervals from about one second to one-sixth of a second, and finds the one-second interval the most favorable. If the interval be irregularly varied within two seconds the effect is hardly noticeable, but if irregularly varied within fifteen seconds the time is increased (Cattell). With a normal re-action to sight of 149σ and to sound of 124σ, the re-action to sight with the interval varying within two seconds was 148σ; when varying within fifteen seconds, to sight 174σ, to sound 165σ (average of two observers). Similarly Martius finds that re-actions with an irregular interval between signal and stimulus result in a time intermediate between that with a regular interval and that without a signal at all. (b) If the time and nature of the stimulus be known, but its *intensity* be varied, the time is increased. When re-acting to a uniform change between a feeble and a loud sound, the re-action time to the former was 127σ, to the latter, 116σ; but when these changes were made in an irregular and unexpected manner, the times were lengthened to 208σ and 198σ.

In a similar manner the attention, which we have supposed hitherto to be focused upon the matter in hand with a maximum of effort, may be prevented from being effectually directed to the making of the re-action by a variety of circumstances. Some of these we may group under the term (2) *distraction*. By a constant noise or other means we may be creating a stimulus to which the attention is involuntarily drawn, and thus withdrawn from the process of re-action. Wundt re-acted to a sound of mean intensity in 189σ, to a strong sound in 158σ, but when a disturbing sound was going on in the room these re-actions required 313σ and 203σ. On the other hand, with Cattell, when in good practice, so that the re-action became almost automatic, the effect of a disturbing sound both upon sight and sound re-actions was insignificant, — normal for sight 149σ, with disturbing noise 155σ; normal for sound 124σ, with dis-

turbing noise 124σ. Dwelshauvers finds a longer re-action
time when a minimum of attention is paid to the re-action.
It is quite probable that what acts as a disturbance to one
person hardly affects another. In some individuals the re-
action time seems to be extremely sensitive to any mental
disturbance. One of Obersteiner's subjects, with an average
re-action time of about 100σ, requires 142σ to re-act when
music is heard, and another's re-action time is lengthened by
100σ when talking is going on in the room.

A more general and thorough form of distraction may be
effected by imposing a task requiring distinct mental effort
at the same time that the re-action is to take place. Thus
Cattell attempted to add 17 consecutively to a series of numbers, and found that re-actions taken while this was going
on were longer by 28σ (average of two observers). All such
effects seem to be much more marked when the re-action in
question is new than when it has become familiar and partly
automatic. The disturbance seems to act by delaying the
association between stimulus and movement.

(3) We have now to notice a distinction which, though
but recently brought to light (by N. Lange, 1888), is of fun-
damental importance. A re-action may be made in two
ways. In the one form of re-action the attention is directed
to the expected impression: it is identified as the expected
impression, and thereupon is initiated the impulse resulting
in the re-acting movement. The several processes are performed serially, the attention being concentrated upon the
sensory part of the process. In the other form of re-action
the attention is directed to the movement: the impulse is
ready, and is set off by the appearance of the signal almost
automatically, the identification of the actual with the expected impression being omitted. The first is spoken of as
the "complete" or "sensory" mode of re-action; the second,
as the "shortened" or "motor" form. In the experiments
of Lange the simple sensory re-action time to a sound (aver-

age of three persons) was 227σ, motor 123σ; to a visual impression (average of two persons), sensory 290σ, motor 113σ;
to a tactile impression (one person), sensory 213σ, motor
108σ.

These differences, however, seem to be rather extreme.
Münsterberg finds for sound, sensory 162σ, motor 120σ.
Martius finds (average of various experiments) for a " sensory " re action to a sound 161σ, for a " motor" 141σ, but in
two subjects not practised in re-acting 210σ and 111σ.
Dwelshauvers finds a difference as great as between 279σ and
137σ for three subjects.   It should be noted that this difference in the attitude of the subject is not always easy to
maintain, and that it is at times equally difficult to decide
whether a re-action has been " sensory " or " motor."   Undoubtedly transitional modes of re-action occur in which the
attention is not sharply focused on either stimulus or movement, but rather divided between the two; and it may be
that this is the most usual mode of re-action when the distinction is not taken into account.   Both Martius and Dwelshauvers
have recorded the subject's own opinion of the quickness of
each re-action, and the state of his attention at the moment
of re-acting.   The estimate of the relative speed of re-action
seems to be fairly accurate, and those re-actions seem to be
shortest in which the attention of the subject was sharply
focused upon the matter in hand.   A further characteristic
of the motor form of re-action is that its average variation is smaller, i.e., the process is more regular; and that
false re-actions occur, either anticipations of stimulus or
re-actions to some accidental disturbance.   The distinction is important as aiding in the explanation of individual differences, as well as of the path of practice.   The
somewhat conflicting results obtained before this distinction was taken into account might very well be due to
the fact that the one observer re-acted in the one way,
and the other in the other.   Thus the re-action times of

Kries and Auerbach are motor; for they are brief, false re-actions occur, and it is noted that the simple re-actions following re-actions involving distinctions were longer by 41σ and 31σ than before,—a change probably due to a return to a partially sensory mode of re-action. Again, there are doubtless transitional modes between the two, and there are reasons for believing that the path of practice is from the sensory to the motor form of re-action.

The influences that remain to be discussed may be considered under the heads of "practice," "fatigue," "individual differences," and "abnormal variations." (4) *Practice*. As just noticed, the effect of practice is intimately connected with the mode of re-action. It is noticed by almost all writers, but the extent to which it influences the time is very various. The observations make it probable that the effect of practice is most marked at first, and that when once the initial stages are over, the effect of continued practice is small. It is greatest in those persons whose time is longest at first, and seems most influential in acts that are complicated and lie somewhat beyond the realm of daily experience.

When the action is once thoroughly learned, an interval of disuse seems not to affect the time seriously. After not re-acting for three months, Cattell found no essential difference in the time. On the other hand, with some there is a slight newness on beginning each day's work, making the first re-actions of a series rather long (Trautscholdt).

(5) A similar statement may be made of *fatigue:* it has greatest effect upon the complicated, less thoroughly learned processes, and varies with the individual and the mode of re-action. With an automatic simple process its effect is very slow to appear (Cattell . It may enter at any stage of the process, sensory, motor, or central; but the last seems to be the most serious. It appears as a difficulty in keeping one's attention upon the experiment, and thus lengthens the time, and especially the average variation of the experi-

ments. By fatigue is meant the fatigue brought about by the experimenting itself. The time is also affected by general fatigue preceding the experiment. Some individuals are extremely sensitive to influences of this kind.

(6) *Individual Variations.* The fact here to be investigated is the general one that different persons require different times for the performance of the same operations. The difficulty of drilling a company of men to act in concert, whether in military drill or otherwise, springs in part from this difference. It was from this point of view, too, that the time of mental processes was first studied. So long ago as 1795 Maskelyne, the astronomer royal, discharged his assistant because the latter recorded the transit of a star across the wire of the telescope half a second or more later than he himself. Some twenty-five years later Bessel, another astronomer, had his attention called to the point, and upon investigation established the fact that no two observers recorded such transits at precisely the same time. The difference in time between any two observers was usually expressed as an equation, and hence the term "personal equation," which, though strictly applicable only to the differences so found, has assumed a much wider meaning. The individual differences become greater as the process to be performed increases in complexity, and this explains in part why the personal equations as determined by the complicated eye and ear method were so large: with the simpler method of electrical record these differences are much reduced. Besides the differences due to practice and the mode of re-action, there are a large number of minor sources of variation, which as yet are not sufficiently understood to justify a correlation of quick or slow re-action times with definite individual qualities. We may, however, note (*a*) that the time is longer in children than in adults, as has been shown, amongst others, by Binet, who found that children from $3\frac{1}{2}$ to 7 years re-acted in from 440σ to 660σ, when adults required

but 140σ. In the very old the time is longer than in the prime of life. Under the influence of mental or physical fatigue, worry, or slight indisposition, the time has been increased. Obersteiner, Vintschgau, Goldscheider, and others, have incidentally observed these effects, showing an increase of 30σ to 40σ. These variations are related to others, shading over into the abnormal. Under this head may be considered (7) *the action of drugs and re-action times in the insane.* Several of the earlier experimenters made a few observations concerning the effect of drugs. Exner found quite a marked lengthening of the time after drinking wine. Vintschgau and Dietl found that the effect of coffee was to decrease and of morphium to increase the time for a considerable period. The more elaborate researches of Kraepelin show that the effect of amyl, ether, and chloroform is a sudden lengthening of the re-action times, reaching a maximum in a very few minutes, and followed by a rather long period of times slightly shorter than the normal. If a strong dose of the drug be used the lengthening is more considerable and the secondary shortening slighter. Thus Kraepelin, whose normal re-action was 183σ, after a strong inhalation of ether re-acted in 298σ, and in the period of shortening in 170σ; while with a light narcosis the maximum re-action was 223σ, and the shortened re-action 150σ. The effect of alcohol, however, is a brief period of shortened times followed by a long period of lengthened times. This is also found by Orchansky, who, with a normal re-action of 155σ, re-acts in 105σ eight minutes after taking a dose of alcohol, and in 225σ after thirty minutes. The observations of Warren do not yield equally positive results, but do not conflict with those of Kraepelin. Changes in the extent of the average variation have also been observed. On what psychological factors these differences depend it is difficult to say, but the subjective feelings accompanying the lengthened times are a difficulty in keeping the attention upon the matter in hand, and an unwillingness to exert one's self. The evidence afforded by the action of drugs upon these processes is important as indicating the dependence of the re-actions upon physiological conditions. A change of re-action times in insanity has been frequently observed, but the field for individual variation is here very large. It seems probable that in most forms of mental disease, and particularly in melancholia, there is a considerable lengthening of the re-action time, amounting in extreme cases to one half or three-quarters of a second. In the excited forms of disease, such as mania, a shortening has been observed. Obersteiner cites a case of general paralysis in the incipient stages of which the time was 166σ, in a more advanced stage 281σ, in a most advanced stage 451σ. Stanley Hall has found a marked shortening of the time in the hypnotic condition, but his result is not corroborated by others.

Methods of Experimentation.

The chief requisite in these experiments is an apparatus for accurately measuring small intervals of time. The earliest method, still in use, records the vibrations of a tuning-fork upon the quickly-moving smoked surface of a rotating drum, and beneath this the moment of giving the signal and making the response. If a fork making one hundred vibrations per second be used, whole hundredths can be directly counted and smaller fractions estimated. Wundt has constructed a more accurate and specialized instrument in which a fork making five hundred vibrations per second is used. A very much simplified form of apparatus has been devised by Obersteiner, in which the slide holding the record is moved by hand, and the movement of re-action draws the fork off the record; and by Bowditch, in which the fork itself carries the record, and the signal and re-action are indicated by a shifting of the writing point. In the astronomical records clock-work takes the place of a tuning-fork. The objection to these methods is that they necessitate tedious counting of curves. If the rate of the rotating-apparatus is very uniform and frequently tested, one may substitute measuring for counting, but the most convenient apparatus for the purpose is the Hipp chronoscope. This instrument contains a fine clock-work, set in motion by releasing a spring and running for about half a minute. The hands of the two dials, the one indicating tenths and the other thousandths of a second, do not move until drawn away from a set of cogs by the opening or closure of a magnetic circuit, and are stopped again in the same way. By making the usual arrangement whereby the production of the stimulus sets the hands in motion and the re-acting movement brings them to a stand-still, we can read off directly the interval of the re-action time. Unless we can afford to sacrifice accuracy for convenience, a means of controlling the chronoscope is indispensable. This may be done by timing the fall of a ball from a given height and comparing it with the theoretical time. In the apparatus for this purpose supplied with the chronoscope the ball is mechanically released, and the mode of making the circuit is equally defective, so that the error of the control apparatus is probably greater than that of the chronoscope. To obviate this difficulty I make use of a ball held in position by a magnet, and falling from any height up to seven feet, upon the arm of a well-balanced lever, thus securing an instantaneous release. By setting the magnet and ball at different distances we are also enabled to decide whether the error is absolute or relative. It is here necessary to break the current by which the ball falls, and to make the current by which the chronoscope starts at the same moment; this is effected by a key specially devised for the purpose. The chronoscope possesses a regulation for altering its rate when too slow or too fast, but I find it most convenient to make sparing use of this, and apply a correction for each day's determinations as found with the "fall apparatus." Another form of control makes use of a falling hammer, the record being also made with a tuning-fork. A recent device of Ewald combines the two methods by mechanically counting the vibrations of a tuning-fork: a delicate armature is drawn to and released by a magnet with each vibration of the fork, moving the hand of a dial over one of its divisions as it does so. The fork is vibrating constantly, but the making of the signal sends the current into the "interruption-counter," while the re-acting movement again diverts the current away from it. It will record at the rate of one hundred per second. Galton has constructed for ordinary uses a machine in which the signal is given by the release of a rod or pendulum, and the re-acting movement mechanically arrests the fall or swing, a scale of interval being determined for the apparatus empirically. Sanford has devised a simple but not expeditious chronoscope, in which the signal and the response separately set in motion two pendulums of slightly different periods, the re-acting interval being calculated from the number of oscillations occurring before the two are in unison.

The methods of indicating the moment at which the signal appeared and the moment at which the re-acting movement was made are simple. When the record is written on a rotating surface, a point connected with a magnet, and writing a straight line beneath the vibrations of the fork, writes that line at a different level when the signal is given, and returns to the same level when the re-acting movement is made; or the tuning-fork itself may be made to write at a different level during the interval measured. The arrangement by which the level is changed on the record, or the hands are set in motion in the chronoscope at the same instant that the stimulus appears, is equally simple. For sound, the noise of the key by which the circuit is made is generally sufficient, or other sound may be produced by bodies falling upon various surfaces and thereby opening or closing a key. For sight, the impression to which a re-action is to be made may be concealed behind a screen, and the drawing away of this screen at the same time makes or breaks an electric circuit. Frequently the re-actor sits in the dark, and the impression becomes visible only when an electric spark appears, or the spark itself may be the stimulus. For touch, temperature, and taste, a typical device is that of Vintschgau, in which the end of a rod touches the sensitive surface, and the pressure so exerted makes a contact with a delicate metallic blade inserted in the same apparatus. For smell, the movement by which the odor is set free is similarly utilized. The re-acting movement is usually that of pressing an ordinary telegraphic key. Devices have been constructed by which movements of the foot, of the jaw, of the voice and lip, may be similarly noted. For more detailed descriptions consult the references under this head at the end.

Having thus considered the time-relations of a simple re-action, we may proceed, on the line of analysis there laid down, to the consideration of the more complex forms of re-action.

Adaptive Re-actions.

It has been noted that the prominent characteristic of a useful re-action is the adaptation of the response to the excitation by which it was called out. This adaptation involves a recognition of the stimulus, and its association with the movement in question. In this recognition we found it convenient to distinguish between the recognition of the presence and that of the nature of the stimulus; but it may be questioned whether we can recognize the presence except by noting some point of the nature of the stimulus, and whether the noting of this point does not involve its distinction from others. If, in re-acting to a sound, I recognize that it is the stimulus to which I am to re-act, and press the key, does this mean that I know that the stimulus is not a visual or a tactile one, that it is not a higher or a lower, a louder or a feebler, sound? Here, as still more in the analysis to follow, our experimental basis is defective.

Experiment has naturally followed the lines of conven-ience and ready analysis; and as there has been little har-mony in these analyses, and as the one here adopted differs somewhat from those adopted by other writers, it will be difficult to maintain the parallelism between theoretical discussion and the obtained results. If we understand by the simple re-action the mere signalling that a definite, pre designated, and expected stimulus is present, and by an "adaptive" re-action one in which the mode of response depends upon and varies with the nature of the stimulus, we may distinguish several stages of connection between the two, as shown in the schedule at the top of the following page.

I. *A single stimulus with a single mode of re-action.*
II. *Several stimuli with a single mode of re-action.*
    (*a*) The subject *foreknows* the stimulus.
    (*b*) The subject *does not foreknow* the stimulus.
III. *A single stimulus with several modes of re-action.*
IV. *Several stimuli with several modes of re-action.*
    (*a*) The subject foreknows the *stimulus and* al o he re-action.
    (*b*) The subject foreknows the *re-action*, but *not* the stimulus

} SIMPLE RE-ACTIONS.

    (*c*) The subject foreknows *neither stimulus* nor re-action. } ADAPTIVE RE-ACTION.

Or, more simply, if the re-action is foreknown, the process is a simple re-action; if not, it is an adaptive re-action. In addition, in the simple re-action the foreknowledge of the stimulus may be entirely definite, the stimulus always being the same, or there may be a known range of variation or an unknown range of variation; while in the adaptive re-action the possibilities are limited to the latter two.

I. has been fully considered. In II. (*a*) we have a number of different simple re-actions; but, instead of investigating them in separate series, we have different kinds in one series: e.g., a sound, a light, or a touch may appear, it being announced to the subject which it is to be; and he in each case re-acts by pressing the key. The impressions may be more homogeneous, as a series of colors; but in all cases the subject need not appreciate the nature of the stimulus, but simply that a stimulus has appeared. In II. (*b*) the subject knows the possible stimuli, but does not know which is to come next; otherwise the conditions are precisely the same as above. Wundt's experiment with the irregular change between two intensities of sound would belong here, and would indicate that this is an essential factor. In III. the several modes of re-action are necessarily known in advance. Instead of testing the different forms of re-actions in separate series, we have several in one series. For example: we re-act to a sound now with the thumb, then with the forefinger, the subject always knowing in advance what he is to do. In

IV. (a) we are combining into one series different forms of simple re-actions, differing both in stimulus and form of re-action; but the complete re-action (e.g., red color to be re-acted to by middle finger) is announced beforehand. In IV. (b) the subject is told in advance how to re-act, but not what the stimulus is to be. However, in both this and the foregoing case he need not wait to recognize the nature of the stimulus, but re acts as soon as he detects its presence. All these are variations of simple re-action times. When we pass to IV. (c), we have a different, namely, an *adaptive*, re-action. The subject is not told any thing in advance except the association upon which he is to re-act: e.g., if a blue light, with the right hand; if a red light, with the left hand; and so on. The essential difference here is that the subject must first distinguish a certain feature of the nature of the stimulus, in this case the color; then call up the appropriate movement and perform it. A re-action of this kind, there-fore, involves a definite distinction of stimuli, and a choice of movements.

Distinction and Choice.

The mental processes involved in an adaptive re-action, in addition to those involved in the simple re action, are thus a more specific recognition of the stimulus, and a choice between movements. By maintaining all other factors alike, the difference of time of the two modes of re-action measures the combined time of distinction and choice. The first determinations of this nature were made by Donders and his pupils (1865–68). A simple re-action to a light, white or red, was made in 201σ (average of five observers); but an adaptive re-action with the right hand for the one light, and the left hand for the other, in 355σ,— a difference of 154σ. Cattell makes a simple adaptive re-action to two colors in 340σ, his simple re-action time being 146σ, or a difference of 194σ (XI.). Münsterberg re-acts simply with any of the five fingers in 141σ, but re-acts with a definite finger (according as the numbers of the fingers "one," "two," "three," etc., are called) in 195σ longer (XXIV.). Accepting these as values for the combined distinction and choice time under simple conditions, our next step would naturally be to determine how much of the time is due to distinction, how much to choice. This is a difficult step; for we cannot readily determine that a distinction has been made, except by indicating it in the mode of reaction, and we cannot execute a choice except upon the basis of some distinction. The most usual experiment by which it has been attempted to overcome this difficulty consists in re-acting to only a designated one of a group of stimuli, allowing all others to pass without re-action. To take a simple case, let red and blue be the possible stimuli: if red appears, re-act; if blue, do nothing. While this form of experiment is interesting and useful, the inferences from it are not as clear as could be wished. It may be termed the "incomplete adaptive re-action," or briefly the "incomplete re-action." It involves a distinction of the stimulus to be re-acted to, from those not to be re-acted to, and a choice between motion and refraining from action. It seems probable that these processes are respectively easier than a distinction that cannot be anticipated and a choice between two movements; but it seems equally probable that the extent of these differences will vary considerably under different circumstances. If the simple re-action is of the quick, motor form, and the incomplete re-action involves an additional distinction of the stimulus, as well as the choice between motion and rest, the additional time above the simple re-action would be long, and the difference between it and the adaptive re-action short. This is evidently the case with Cattell and Berger, who, with a simple re action of 146σ and 150σ, perform the incomplete re-action in 306σ and 277σ, the adaptive in 340σ and 295σ (IV. and XI.). On the other hand, Donders, with an evidently sensory mode of re-action, has a simple re-action of 201σ, an incomplete of 237σ, and an adaptive of 284σ. A second method attempts to deal with the difficulty by delaying the re-action until the precise nature of the stimulus has been appreciated, and regards the difference in time between this and the simple re-action as the time needed for the distinction of the stimulus. There is nothing but the subjective guaranty that the moment of re-action is coincident with the process of recognition, and we have no reason to regard this guaranty as valid. There may be a tendency to make the distinction on the basis of the after-image, and thus signal the appreciation of it too soon; or, again, an extreme desire not to re-act before the distinction is made may delay re-action to an unusual length. Friederich's investigations show for colors a simple re-action time of 175σ, and a "subjective distinction" time of 267σ (XXXIX.); while Tigerstedt, and also Tischer, find only about half this difference for nearly the same re-action. It seems wisest, under these circumstances, not to decide the relative shares of the distinction and choice in the adaptive re-action, but to study the combined time as a whole, and the influences by which it is affected. We can thus utilize the results of all the methods for comparative purposes; and, in addition, we can vary the complexity of the distinction while leaving the choice the same (and to a more limited extent can vary the choice without the distinction), and thus can in many cases distinguish whether an increased complexity of an adaptive re-action is to be referred to an increase in the difficulty of the choice or to an increase in the difficulty of the distinction.

It is desirable to analyze more particularly the nature of the difference between the simple re-action and the "subjective," and between the simple and the incomplete. An essential point relates to the mode of re-action, whether motor or sensory; nor is it necessary that the same mode of re-action be followed in all cases. A few points here relevant are illustrated in Tischer's results upon nine subjects with sound re-actions and distinctions. The average of the nine gives a distinction time of 159σ, and a simple time of 118σ. Four of the subjects evidently make use of the motor re-action, their simple time being 107σ, and their subjective distinction 116σ; i.e., the re-action takes place upon the appearance of the stimulus, its distinction taking place later. Berger and Cattell express the same difficulty, and for this reason discarded the method. Their simple re-action to weak light was 198σ, with distinction of intensity 208σ. Two of the subjects evidently re-act according to the "sensory" method, their simple re-action being 141σ, and the subjective distinction 246σ. That these are not individual differences is shown by the fact that the adaptive re-actions are about alike in all. Similarly with regard to the difference between the simple and the incomplete re-action times. Donders, and those of Tischer's subjects who re-act by the "sensory" method, show a relatively small difference, though this is not true of Friederich's subjects. While Tischer's "motor" subjects show a difference of 159σ between the simple and the incomplete, the "sensory" subjects show one of only 61σ. Again, when the re-action is "motor," the expectation is entirely directed to the stimulus upon which re-action is to follow, and the fact that other stimuli may appear hardly enters into the experiment. This seems to be the case with Kries and Auerbach, who, with clearly "motor" re-actions, find a difference of 30–40σ for (XXX.–XXXVI.) a variety of incomplete re-actions. It may be added that the change from the simple to the incomplete form of re-action will often bring with it an attention to the sensory part of the process, and thus make the difference between it and the simple time long. This seems to be the case with Berger and Cattell, who, with a simple re-action time of 147σ and 150 σ, have an incomplete re-action time of 306 σ and 277σ. The difference between the incomplete and the adaptive re-action seems to be uniformly small (many of the differences being not far from 40σ), though the individual variations are considerable. It is likely that the effects attributed to practice and fatigue may really be due to a change from the sensory to the motor form of re-action. Thus Kries and Auerbach mention that their incomplete times were at first very long, but that they became very small, the reduction continuing long after the effect of practice upon the simple re-action had ceased. Again, the fact

Table of Complex Re-action Times.[1]

No.	Nature of Distinction. Between.	Character of Experiment.	Nature of Re-action.	Observer.	TIME.	Simple Re-action Time.	No. of Possible Impressions.	Remarks.
I	Black and white-on-black.	Incomplete.	Finger.	Cattell.	241	146	?	Re-act to white-on-black.
II	White and a particular color.	"	"	"	249	146	?	Re act to color, varied amongst ten.
III	White and a color.	"	"	"	264	146	?	Re-act to color, but need not distinguish same.
IV	Red:blue or green:yellow	"	"	"	306	146	?	Re-act to predesignated color
V	Colors	"	"	"	313	146	10	"
VI	Roman capital letters	"	"	"	326	146	26	" letter
VII	Short English words	"	"	"	360	146	26	" word (printed).
VIII	Long "	"	"	"	375	146	26	" "
IX	Short German "	"	"	"	367	146	26	" "
X	Pictures of objects	"	"	"	309	146	26	" picture.
XI	Red:blue or green:yellow	Adaptive.	{ Right & left hand. Naming.	"	310	146	?	
XII	Pairs of short English words	"	"	"	401	170	?	5 sets. Average of re-actions to all.
XIII	" " colors	"	"	"	438	170	?	"
XIV	" " pictures	"	"	"	435	170	?	"
XV	Capital Roman letters	"	"	"	421	170	26	
XVI	" German letters	"	"	"	526	170	26	
XVII	Short English words	"	"	"	409	170	26	
XVIII	" German "	"	"	"	439	170	26	
XIX	Colors	Continuous series.	"	"	601	170	10	
XX	Pictures of objects		"	"	515	170	26	
XXI	Words in construction		"	"	138	170	Indefinite.	English.
XXII	" "		"	"	250	170	?	German. read backward
XXIII	" "		"	"	288	170	?	English, (right to left).
XXIV	Spoken words, "one," "two," "three,""four,""five"	Adaptive.	5 fingers.	Münsterberg.	383	162	5	Sensory.
XXV	" words, "luns,""luni"							"

XXVI	Spoken words, 5 groups of 5 grammatical forms.	Adaptive.	5 fingers.	Münsterberg.	688	162	5	"Du deiner dir dich ihr. (Der des dem den die.
XXVII	" words, 5 categories...	"	"	"	712	162	5	" Noun, pronoun, adjective, number, verb.
XXVIII	" " "	"	"	"	893	162	5	" City, river, animal, plant, element.
XXIX	" " "	"	"	"	1122	162	5	" Author, musician, natural-ist, philosopher, statesman.
XXX	Direction of light............	Incomplete.	Finger.	Kries and Auerbach.	209	195	2	Whether right or left spark goes first.
XXXI	Colors......	"	"	"	227	209	?	Whether in front or in back of fixation-point.
XXXII	Distance of points	"	"	"	2 3	177	?	On middle finger or back of hand.
XXXIII	Localize touch...........	"	"	"	161	132	2	Re-act to higher.
XXXIV	Tones of different pitch	"	"	Friedo-rich's 3 subjects.	177	143	2	" strong.
XXXV	Tone and noise......	"	"	"	176	142	?	" lower.
XXXVI	Strong and weak touch......	"	"	"	176	134	2	" weak.
XXXVII	Tones of different pitch......	"	"	"	202	158	2	
XXXVIII	Strong and weak touch......	"	"	"	219	140	2	
XXXIX	White and black......	Subjective.	"	"	267	175	?	
XL	White, black, red, green.....	"	"	"	296	175	4	Read.
XLI	One-place numbers	"	"	"	318	186	9	"
XLII	Three-place "	"	"	"	397	186	900	
XLIII	Five-place "	"	"	"	637	186	Indefinite.	
XLIV	Sounds of different intensity	"	"	Tischer's 6 subjects.	146	114	2	
XLV	" "	"	"	"	164	114	3	
XLVI	" "	"	"	"	178	114	4	
XLVII	" "	"	"	"	194	114	5	
XLVIII	Visual impressions.........	Adaptive.	2-10 fingers	Merkel's 10 subjects.	276	188	2	Any two of the numbers 1, 2, 3, 4, 5, and I., II., III., IV., V.
XLIX	" "	"	"	"	294	188	4	" four of the Nos. 1, 2, etc.
L	" "	"	"	"	489	188	6	" six " "
LI	" "	"	"	"	562	188	8	" eight " "
LII	" "	"	"	"	588	188	10	The ten numbers
LIII	100 words......	Contin. ser.	Naming.	Cattell.	255	—	—	
LIV	100 letters	"	"	"	224	—	—	

¹ Roman numerals in the text refer to the corresponding experiments in this table.

that simple re-action times are long when following complex ones, or that subjective times are longer when following adaptive re-actions, seems to be not so much the effect of fatigue as of a continuance of a sensory mode of re-action. It should also be mentioned that Tigerstedt ingeniously proposes to measure the distinction time by taking the difference between two incomplete re-actions, in one of which we re-act to a definite simple impression, and in the other to the impression requiring distinction (e.g., in one series I re-act to white, but not to a color; in the other, to a color, but not to white); and the difference in time will be needed for distinguishing a color from white. The general fact re mains, then, that while the combined distinction and choice times exhibit only such individual and other variations as seem explicable by the differences in the conditions of experiment (the adaptive re action times of eight of Tischer's nine subjects fall between 293 and 320σ), the estimates that have been attempted of the portions of the time due to distinction and to choice separately, show such large variations as to force the conviction that the different experimenters were not measuring the same processes.

Conditions affecting Distinction and Choice.

Bearing in mind that we are dealing with comparative results only, and comparisons restricted mainly to the results of the same observer, obtained by the same method, we proceed to investigate the conditions by which these processes involving distinction and choice are affected. It will be convenient to begin with the effect of (1) *the number of distinctions and of choices.* The effect of the number of objects among which distinction is to take place, upon the time needed to make the distinction, is best shown in the "incomplete" and subjective methods, in which the range of distinction may be varied without affecting that of choice. For example: Cattell makes an incomplete re-action to a certain color when either that or one other color may appear in 306σ, when either that or any one of nine other colors may appear (IV and V.) in 313σ. Friederich's subjects make a subjective distinction between two colors in 267σ, between four in 296σ (XXXIX. and XL.). Six of Tischer's subjects make a subjective distinction between two sounds of different intensity in 146σ (simple re-action, 114σ); between three sounds, in 164σ; four sounds, in 178σ; five sounds, in 194σ (XLIV.-XLVII.). Other experiments cited in the table (p. 32) show the same slight increase of distinction time with the increase of the range of impressions, but complicated with other factors as well. With regard to the effect upon the choice time when the number of possible choices increases, we have the results of Merkel, who found for the simple re-action time of ten subjects to visual impressions 188σ; for an adaptive re-action between two impressions, 276σ; between three, 330σ; between four, 394σ; between five, 415σ; between six, 489σ; between seven, 526σ; between eight, 562σ; between nine, 581σ; and between ten, 588σ (partially cited in XLVIII.-LII.). The impressions were the numbers 1, 2, 3, 4, 5, and I., II., III., IV., and V. The re-actions to movements of the ten fingers naturally associated with these impressions, and the naturalness of this association doubtlessly contributes to the small increase in time. Münsterberg *called* these numbers and re-acted in the same way, finding for a choice between five movements 383σ, and between ten 478σ (simple re-action being 162σ). Martius finds for the same re-actions 474σ and 552σ (average of three observers). It being established that but a small share of the increase is due to the distinction (Merkel has experimentally shown this for his subjects), we may conclude, that, with an increase in number, the difficulty of choice increases more rapidly than the difficulty of distinction. In addition, we have reason to believe that the increase would be still more marked in case the association between impression and motion is artificial. When this association reaches the maximum of naturalness, in naming objects, the increase with the number of impressions is slight. Thus it may be calculated from Cattell's results that it takes him but about

10σ longer to name 26 letters or short words than to name
one of two, but 60σ longer to name one of 26 than one of
two pictures, and 163σ longer to name one of ten than one
of two colors; the action of naming being more closely related to letters and words than to pictures and colors.

It is the ability to deal promptly and correctly with a large
and varying number of impressions, disposing of each in its
appropriate way, that we recognize as evidence of mental
power, and it is this that experiment shows to be a factor
of great influence upon the time of an adaptive re-action.
It is the skill in disposing of so large a number of adaptive
re-actions that we admire in the post-office clerk, and in many
other exhibitions of manual dexterity. It is this that necessi-
tates the division of labor, there being a limit to the number
of adaptive re-actions that can be economically controlled.
Again: the fact that a large number of distinctions does not
complicate the process as much as a large number of choices,
finds its analogue in the observation that our power of re-
production falls below our powers of appreciation. This
plays a part in the fact that we learn to understand a language long before we learn to speak it, and in many similar
processes. The development of mental power reveals itself
as an increasing facility in performing a large number of
complicated adaptive re-actions; and here, too, the power
of appreciating distinctions develops earlier than the power of
choosing. This result was illustrated experimentally in a
brief study of the re-action times of a ten-year-old child as
compared with those of an adult. While the pure distinction time rose from 58σ to 250σ as the impressions to be
distinguished increased from two to five (subjective method,
with colors), as compared with 44σ and 78σ for adults, for
the adaptive re-action for two impressions the time was 120σ,
for five impressions 603σ, as compared with 79σ and 210σ
for adults.

We may conveniently introduce the general topic of the

effect of the nature of the distinction and the choice upon
the time of its performance with the consideration of a few
points affecting the distinction alone. (2) *The similarity
of the impressions.* The endowment of the various sense-
organs varies considerably (e.g., the sense of musical pitch is
finer than that of sound intensity); but, in the absence of a
standard of comparison of sense-differences in disparate types
of sensation, we can only illustrate the point in question by
varying the difficulty of distinction within the same sense.
Thus Kries and Auerbach find that it takes much longer to
tell whether a sound is to the right or to the left, according
as the two points at which the sound is produced are closer
together. When they form an angle of 35°–120° with the
centre of the face, the additional time (by the incomplete
method) was 17σ; when varied between 35° and 26°, the
time was 78σ; when within 26° and 11°, it was 137σ. The
ease of distinction is largely a function of practice. We
readily seize the slight optical differences furnished by the
different letters of a known language, but constantly con-
fuse much greater sense-differences with which we are less
familiar. (3) *The specific nature of the impression.* Very
many of the results cited in the table may be said to illustrate the effect of a change in the nature of the distinction;
but it is difficult to show this, uncomplicated with other
variations. The determinations of Kries and Auerbach
(XXX.–XXXVIII.) show the result of distinctions of various kinds, though an analysis of the causes of these differences is hardly practicable. It is quite clear that in re-acting by the incomplete method the re-action is shorter when
the stimulus is the stronger of two intensities than when it
is the weaker of the two (XXXVI and XXXVIII.). Berger
has also shown that the intensity of the stimulus has some
influence upon the distinction time beyond what would be
due to the effect upon the simple re-action time therein con-
tained. The difference between the corresponding simple

and the incomplete re-action to a bright light is 85σ; to a medium light, 119σ; to a weak light, 114σ; while similar differences for adaptive re-actions are 167σ, 179σ, 192σ; the inference being that the intensity of the stimulus affects the distinction rather than the choice. Again (in the series VI.–X.), we find that Cattell recognized most quickly that an expected one of 26 pictures was present, then that one of 26 letters, next one of 26 short English words, next one of 26 short German words. The differences between the time for recognizing letters and short words is very slight compared to the increase in complexity of the impression, and thus shows the effect of practice in recognizing words as a whole. Furthermore, in the series of experiments (partly cited in XLI.–XLIII.) in which one to six place numbers were recognized, while there is a concomitant increase in the number of possible impressions, it seems fair to refer the main increase in time to the increasing complexity of the impression. In passing from the recognition of one to two or of two to three place numbers, the increase in time is slight; but from there on, the increase itself increases with the increase of the number of numerals (53σ, 147σ, 322σ),— a fact probably related to the practice in grasping numbers in groups of threes. Another series (XXIV.–XXIX.) may be mentioned here, and is interesting as indicating that it is more difficult to tell to which of five categories (a *city*, a *river*, etc.) a word belongs than what part of speech it is; and this is in turn easier than to tell the sphere of activity of a noted man. It should be noted that the choice, the range of impressions, the connection between impression and movement, the method of re-action, are equivalent in all three experiments; so that the difference is fairly referable to the distinction process involved. We may finally notice as here pertinent the observations of Vintschgau upon the distinguishability of different tastes. He found that by the incomplete method it took longest to re-act to bitter when the alternative was distilled water, next long to sweet, next to sour, and shortest to salt. Similarly, in adaptive re-actions with the two hands to all possible combinations of two of the four tastes, salt was most quickly re-acted to (384σ), sour next (397σ), sweet next (409σ), and bitter last (456σ).

(4) *The Foreknowledge of the Subject.* Within the re-striction that the foreknowledge of the subject shall be limited to the knowledge of the associative bond between stimulus and movement, there is room for variation. The simplest case would present but one stimulus re-acted to, and but one not re-acted to, or, in the adaptive re-action, but one stimulus for each mode of re-action. In all such cases (I., II., IV., XI., XXXVIII., may be cited as instances) the foreknowledge of the subject presents the maximum of definiteness. Any departure from these conditions brings with it an increase in the time of re-action. Cattell finds but a very slight increase ($5-7\sigma$) in the incomplete re-action when the stimulus *not re-acted to*, instead of being but a single one, is any one of ten colors, but finds a greater increase (15σ, difference of II. and III.) when the stimulus *re-acted to*, instead of being a single one, is one of ten colors, though the particular kind of color need not be recognized. Both the stimulus re-acted to and the one not re-acted to might be one of a larger or smaller, a more or less homogeneous group; but I am unable to find a record of such an experiment. The somewhat modified form of experiment adopted by Tigerstedt and Bergqvist shows a similar result. They re-acted to a light, when either the light or a one to three place number might appear, in 297σ, and to the number (including its recognition) in 318σ. If the number of digits of the numbers that may appear is foreknown, the time is considerably reduced; and when either the light or a foreknown letter might appear, the time for recognizing the light was still further shortened (190σ). The same series of variations could be applied to adaptive re-actions (i.e., one

or more, or all, of the modes of re-action might be associated
with any member of a variable group of stimuli), but experiments designed to show the effect of such variations are
lacking.   Mention should be made, however, of the experiments of Münsterberg, in which he first re-acts with the five
fingers to five categories, each limited to one term (XXIV.
and XXV.); then to five categories, each comprising three
terms (XXVI.); and then to five categories, each comprising a practically indefinite number of terms (XXVII.,
XXVIII., XXIX.); and finds an increase of time in making
these steps (Martius has repeated experiments XXV.,
XXVI., and XXVII., finding the times to be 551σ, 644σ,
and 804σ).   Although other factors contribute to this increase in time, part of it may be referred to the decreasing
definiteness of the foreknowledge of the subject.   It may be
added, that the mechanism by which an increase in the
number of possible re-actions increases the re-action time
is allied to that by which a decrease in the foreknowledge of
the subject does so.

The effect of the *mode of re-action* upon the re-action
time is the same here as in the simple re-action.   Re-acting
by the voice in the incomplete form of re-action has been
found to be longer than re-acting by the finger; and whenever the re-action takes the form of speaking or naming, it
takes some time to place the organs in position and speak
the word.   But a very special and important effect in adaptive re-actions is that of (5) *the association between movement and stimulus.*

As the effect of a special or a general practice, certain
modes of re-acting to certain types of stimuli have become
natural, easy, and familiar, while in other cases (e.g., the
re-acting by pressing a key, — a process learned only for the
purposes of the experiment) the association is extremely
artificial   If we compare, in Münsterberg's series, the experiment in which the five fingers re act to the numbers

"one," "two," "three," "four," "five" (XXIV.), with
that in which they re-act to the declensional forms of a Latin
noun (XXV.), we recognize that the former is a more natural association than the latter, and seem justified in at-
tributing a good share of the increase in time to this difference. Again: to re-act by naming is a process in which we
have had considerable training, and it is quite evident that
the time needed for naming one of 26 different impressions
(XV.–XVIII., and XX.) is much shorter than would be
needed for re acting by 26 artificial and irregular movements
of the hand. The difficulty in learning a foreign language,
or a telegraphic code, or a shorthand system of writing, is
largely the difficulty of forming associations between complex stimuli and movements; and the great decrease in time
that is brought about when such associations have been
mastered emphasizes the importance of the factor now under
discussion, which, in turn, may be regarded as an expression
of the effect of practice.

We may push the analysis a step farther. The process of
naming is much more closely associated with a word or a
letter than with a picture or a color; for the former are
artificial symbols, becoming significant only when so
interpreted, while the latter reveal their meaning directly
without needing to be named or read. Accordingly, we find
that it takes longer to name a color (601σ) or a picture
(545σ) than to name a letter (424σ) or a word (409σ), though
the recognition of a color or a picture is a quicker process
than the recognition of a letter or a word (compare XV.,
XVII., XIX., XX., and V., VI., VII., X). Furthermore,
if the time of naming or reading is thus mainly conditioned
by the strength of association involved, we may in turn
utilize this process as an index of familiarity with the naming or reading, or, more briefly, with the language. Thus
Cattell, an American, reads English words more quickly
than German (XVII. and XVIII.), while with Berger, a

German, this relation is reversed. To name a picture in German occupies Cattell for 614σ; in English, 588σ. It occupies Berger in German for 501σ; in English, 580σ. The inference is the same (though the absolute time is much shorter) if we read words in construction instead of isolated. By this method Cattell finds that he can read an English word in 138σ, a French in 167σ, a German in 250σ, an Italian in 327σ, a Latin in 434σ, and a Greek word in 484σ, this being the order of his familiarity with these languages. The particular nature of the association may be revealed in the study of these time-relations. Thus, while in all cases it takes longer to read words from right to left than from left to right, this difference is relatively least in the least familiar languages; i.e., in those in which the bond of association between the words is least significant. For a like reason letters are read much more quickly from above downwards (102σ) than from below upwards (264σ).

(6) *The Overlapping of Mental Processes.* We pass now to a point of critical importance in the application of results gained in the laboratory, to the mental operations of daily life. While in the former case we are performing a set task, isolated for purposes of investigation, in the latter case (i.e., in such operations as reading, copying, playing upon instruments, and the like) we are performing a continuous, more or less extended, series of re-actions, bound together by bonds of common purpose and associations of habit. It is not a mere aggregate, but an organization of mental processes: and this makes possible the performance of the several factors of the process in part at the same time. It leads to an "overlapping" of the mental elements. It is a proficiency in thus doing several things at once that constitutes much of the difference between the expert and the novice; and it is this "telescoping" process that seems to be the method by which complicated operations are at length performed in short times. It is for this reason that the time

per word of reading 100 words is shorter than the time of reading a single word. Cattell reads a short word in 409σ, a long one in 451σ, but 100 such in 255σ per word, and, if the words are in construction, in 125σ per word; thus indicating how much of the difference between ordinary reading, and reading single words, is due to the continuity of the experiment, how much to the association between the words. So, also, Cattell reads a single letter in 424σ, but 100 such in 224σ (compare XVII., XV., with LIII., LIV.). When the series is too long continued, fatigue sets in, and the time is again longer; it is longer for 500 than for 100 words and letters; and for colors and pictures there is no saving in naming 100 above naming a single color or picture.

A special study of this power of grasping several things at once was made by Cattell by having letters move along on the surface of a rotating drum, and varying the width of a slit in a screen through which they were read. When the slit just allowed one letter to be seen at a time, they could be read at the rate of one letter in 228σ; and as the slit was widened to admit two, three, four, five, and six letters at once, the rate increased to one letter in 200σ, 178σ, 166σ, 160σ, and 160σ. As it takes 424σ to name a letter singly (XV.), it would seem that the whole of a letter need not be seen at once to be recognized,—an inference corroborated by the fact, that, when the slit admits only one-tenth of a letter at a time, the letters can be read at 400σ per letter. The result also indicates that there is a limit to the power in question. M. Paulhan finds similar results in more complex operations. He multiplies numbers and recites a verse or two at the same time; and the time needed for this is shorter than the sum of the times required to do each separately. In very simple cases the time of doing both together is not longer than the time for doing the more difficult of the two separately. The mind should accordingly not be likened to a point at which but a single object can impinge at one time, but rather to a surface of variable extension. It should likewise be noted that the performance of a complex and extended mental task is not the same thing as the separate performance of the several elements into which that task may be analyzed.

Münsterberg has applied the distinction between the *sensory* and *motor* form of re-action to complicated adaptive re-actions, and regards it as there involving the overlapping of mental processes. The times cited in the table (XXIV.-XXIX.) in Münsterberg's experiments refer to sensory re-actions. In these the attention is directed to the word about to be uttered. It is recognized, and referred to its group. The corresponding movement is then aroused and performed, the several processes being successive in time. In the motor form the word is thought of as a "forefinger-moving" word; and the movement upon which the attention is kept fixed is expectantly kept ready to be set off at the slightest notice. The several processes thus play into one another, some perhaps entirely falling away. Both anticipatory movements and errors (moving the finger next to the correct one) are not infrequent. The motor times for the series XXIV.-XXIX. are 289, 355, 430, 432, 432, and 437σ; the differences between motor and sensory times, 94, 110, 258, 280, 461, 685σ. Until these very important and striking results are better understood, it would be unwise to enter into a discussion of them. Martius has very recently repeated some of Münsterberg's results (XXIV.-XXVII.), and not only fails to corroborate them, but finds that the attention to the movement about to be made *lengthens* the time. He holds that the distinction between motor and sensory re-actions is applicable only to simple re-actions, and, while unable to explain Münsterberg's results, does not believe the difference there involved to be the same as that involved in simple re-actions. It remains for future research to shed light upon the problem.

(7) *Practice and Fatigue.* What was said under these headings of simple re-actions applies with equal force to complex ones. Various experimenters notice the decrease in time as the experiments proceed. They note that this

decrease is relatively greatest at first, and in those individuals and processes whose time is relatively longest at the out-
set; also that it soon reaches a limit, and, when once thoroughly acquired, is not liable to be lost after a moderate
degree of disuse; and that it at times seems to be confused
with a transition from a sensory to a motor form of re-action. As illustrative of one or other of these points, it may
be mentioned that Tischer finds as a rather typical case the
decrease of a distinction time from 160σ in the first set to
95σ in the second, and 86σ in the third, all reduction ceas-
ing on the average after 5.5 sets; that Trautscholdt, in re-
actions consisting of repeating a word, finds times of 299,
273, and 258, and in another case of 205, 176, and 155σ, in
three successive periods of fourteen days each; that Berger and Cattell, beginning with some practice in experiments of this kind, find the time for incomplete re-actions
reduced by 30 and 20σ after four months' experimentation;
and, finally, that the great decrease in the incomplete re-
actions of Kries and Auerbach (from 64 and 117 to 21σ,
from 153 and 109 to 36σ, from 104 and 97 to 49 and 54σ, in
various experiments) strongly suggests a radical change in the
mode of re-action. Another aspect of the effect of practice
appears in a study by Berger of the times required by the
boys of the nine classes of a German Gymnasium, and of
the class preparatory to the Gymnasium, to read 100 and
500 words in construction in German and in Latin at a
maximum and at a normal rate. There is a constant decrease in time as the boys advance in age. In Latin the several
times per word were 262, 135, 100, 84, 79, 57, 54, 49, 48, 43σ;
in German 72, 55, 43, 37, 39, 28, 27, 26, 25, 23σ; the great
difference between the first two times in Latin being due to
the fact that the boys who required 262σ to read a Latin
word had never learned Latin at all. That these differences
are to be referred to specific practice rather than to general
mental maturity, appears from a comparison of the above

times with the times required by those boys to name colors; viz., 135, 99, 119, 123, 100, 91, 112, 99, 86 σ.

The results regarding fatigue are not equally definite. Many mention the general fact of fatigue, and to avoid it perform but few experiments in a series. We have already seen that it takes relatively longer to read 500 letters, words, colors, pictures, than to read 100. On the other hand, Cattell, after a very long series of re-actions, found no serious or constant increase in the time, but seemed to feel the effects of fatigue on the following day. Both practice and fatigue are subject to large individual variations. Oehrn has studied the minor variations of practice and fatigue in a session of two hours' work, finding first a stage in which practice outweighs fatigue, and then a stage in which the reverse is true.

(8) *Miscellaneous and Individual Variations.* The complex re-actions, just as the simple ones are subject to the influences of distraction, vary under the action of drugs, in morbid conditions, and present large individual variations. These points, though frequently noticed incidentally, have not been subjected to special study, so that briefly citable and conclusive figures are lacking. Regarding the action of drugs, Kraepelin is inclined to believe that the distinction is, under their influence, almost always rendered more difficult, being only slightly subject to the period of shortened times, while the choice factor very readily becomes shorter than the normal. Marie Walitzkaja finds that the complex re-action times in the insane differ more from the normal than do their simple times. An adaptive re-action for the two hands which for the normal required 351–406 σ, required 707–943 σ in cases of general paralysis, and 1085 σ in a case of mania. These should, however, be regarded as individual rather than general results. The individual variations may be regarded as increasing with the complexity of the re-action. Men differ more from one another in the time

needed for doing difficult things than in the time needed for simple things. Systematic experimentation upon this point is lacking: but a suggestion of the truth may be obtained by calculating the average deviation from their mean, of Merkel's ten subjects in their simple re-action times, their subjective distinction times, and their adaptive re-action times; the result being 2.23 per cent, 3.35 per cent, and 6.79 per cent.

Association Times.

While the effect of the association between stimulus and movement upon the time of the re-action has been already discussed, the process of association forms so important a factor in our mental life, that it requires a more specialized and independent investigation.

(1) *Questions with but a Single Answer.* We may view an adaptive re-action under the aspect of a "question and answer;" the stimulus being equivalent to the question, "What, with regard to certain points, is this impression?" and the answer, whether indicated by a name, or word, or movement, is given in the re-action. Our problem is to investigate the time-relations of these questions and answers, as an index of the readiness of the association between the two. The processes intervening between the appreciation of the question and the formulation of the answer may vary greatly in complexity and character. A common characteristic of the re-actions hitherto regarded consisted in the fact that the material for forming the answer is simply and directly supplied by the stimulus itself: it is in the main a verdict regarding the particular nature of sensation then present. The re-actions to which we now pass all include something more than this; and the formulation of the answer involves to a greater or less extent more complicated forms of mental activity, and depends more or less upon the past experiences, the special habits and tendencies of mind, of the individual.

While the line of division between the direct appreciation
and the indirect interpretation of a sense-impression cannot
be rigidly drawn, and while it is no less difficult to decide
what processes are involved in this interpretation and elaboration of the sense-impression, yet we may with sufficient
precision mark out as the first class of associations ⟨ a⟩ those
in which *a simple act of memory* plays the chief *rôle*.
Thus, when Cattell, instead of naming a picture in his own
language (which he does in 545σ), names it in German (in
694σ), the difference in time is needed for calling to mind
the German name, and measures the strength of this association. Berger's acquaintance with English is less than
Cattell's with German, and accordingly with him the difference between naming a picture in the vernacular and in a
foreign language is greater (477σ and 649σ). The translation of a short familiar word from English to German occupies Cattell 686σ; from German to English, but 580σ; the
time for long and less familiar words being much longer.
(We may obtain the portion of the time required for the act
of translation alone by subtracting from this the time to see
and name a word, 428σ.) Such operations as addition and
multiplication, when confined to numbers of one place, can
hardly be more than acts of memory. Cattell adds such
numbers in 336σ; Berger, who is a mathematician, in 221σ.
The former multiplies them in 544σ; the latter, in 389σ.
Vintschgau's three subjects multiply such numbers (though
under different conditions) in 233σ. More complicated types
of "memory re-actions" have been performed by Cattell and
by Münsterberg. The former determined in separate series
the time necessary, when given a city, to name the country
in which it was situated (462σ); when given a month, to
name the season to which it belongs (310σ), to name the following month (389σ), to name the preceding month (832σ);
given an author, to name the language in which he wrote
(350σ); given an eminent man, to name his sphere of activity

(368σ). Münsterberg constantly varied the type of question including such as the above, the position of cities, the qualities of objects, the relations of men, and many others, finding an average time of 848σ (average of two subjects). While many of these determinations are doubtless of more individual than general value, we may stop to note a few points that are presumably typical. The re-actions here grouped under one class vary considerably in difficulty, and a few instances may be cited to indicate the range of this variation. In giving a country in which a given city is situated, the shortest time is for Paris (278σ); the longest, for Geneva (485σ). In giving the language in which an author wrote, Berger requires least time for Luther (227σ) and Goethe (265σ), most for Bacon (565σ); Cattell, least for Plato (224σ) and Shakspeare (258σ), most for Plautus (478σ). In giving the calling of an eminent man, the least time is required for poets (291σ), the longest for men of science (421σ). Münsterberg mentions as quickly answered questions (400σ to 600σ), "On what river is Cologne?" "In what season is June?" "In what continent is India?" as questions requiring a long time (1100σ –1300σ), "Who is the author of Hamlet?" "What is the color of ice?" "Who was the teacher of Plato?" An influence which we have found of great significance hitherto is equally important here; viz., the foreknowledge of the subject of what is to occur. In Cattell's experiments the general question is virtually asked once for the entire series, the special terms being given in each experiment, while in Münsterberg's results the entire question changes with each observation; and this difference in the expectancy of the subject cannot but be an important factor in the longer times found by the latter. A somewhat different phase of this influence appears in the results of Vintschgau. In multiplying the numbers from 1×1 to 9×9, the smaller number was always announced first. Accordingly, when the first nine was announced, the subject practically anticipated the result, and had the product ready; when eight was announced, he knew that it was one of two results; when seven, one of three; and so on. Accordingly we find these to be the shortest processes (9×9, only 160σ) but there is another factor at work counteracting this effect, viz., the familiarity of certain multiplications, making the products by *one* short, and those by four and five long.

(*b*) The next type of "question and answer" will be one in which, in addition to the act of memory, a *comparison*, or a *judgment*, is involved. The result of the comparison, though not always the same for all individuals (and in this sense the question is not limited to a single answer), will probably always be the same in the same individual. The only experiment of Cattell's that seems properly to belong here is that in which the subject decided which was the greater of two eminent men (558σ). Münsterberg finds the average time for answering a miscellaneous group of such comparisons 947σ, or 99σ longer than the process without comparison: comparisons rapidly made (600σ-800σ) being, "Which has the more agreeable odor,—cloves or violets?" "Who is greater,—Virgil or Ovid?" "What is more beautiful,—woods or mountain?" and difficult questions (1200σ-1500σ) being, "Which is healthier,—swimming or dancing?" "Which do you like better,—Goethe's drama or his lyric?" "Which is more difficult,—physics or chemistry?" The comparison may be among more than two objects. Thus, in asking which is the finest of Goethe's dramas, the process of formulating the reply may include the calling to mind what the various dramas are, and a choice among them; not, of course, a considerate judgment, but the selection, under the necessity of an immediate answer, of one deciding motive. On the other hand, among the several possibilities, a certain one may, by habitual association or for other reasons, have become so prominent that virtually no comparison ensues; and the relatively slight excess in time of this type of association above the former ones (1049σ) suggests that this was often the case.   To decide which is the pleasantest odor (rose), or which the most important German river (Rhine), required only between 600σ and 700σ; to decide which was the most difficult Greek author (Pindar), or your favorite French writer (Corneille), from 1400σ to 1600σ.

Münsterberg has ingeniously modified this form of experiment to show the influence of the foreknowledge or preparedness of the subject.   He precedes the asking of the question by a dozen or so words of the category within which the comparison is to be made.   Thus, "Apples, pears, cherries, peaches, plums, grapes, strawberries, dates, figs, raisins: which do you like better,—grapes or cherries?" Although the comparison cannot be begun until the last word is heard, still the subject has in a way anticipated the general nature of the question, as well as the scope of the comparison, and has reduced the time considerably (676σ, as compared with 947σ),—certainly a striking result.

(2) *Questions with More than a Single Answer.*   In the class of re-actions to which we now pass, the question admits of several answers.   The answer at one time may not be the same as at another time; and the determining factors in the particular character of the answer are the peculiar mental habits and tendencies of the individual. The question thus changes from a specific to a general one, the answer being any member of a more or less extended class answering to such and such a description.   In some the choice may be somewhat limited.   This is true of Cattell's experiments in which, given a country, we are to name a city in it (346σ); given a season, to name a month in it (435σ); given a language, to name an author writing in that language (519σ); or, given an author, to name any work of his (763σ).   In all these cases we are apt to have in mind only a very few prominent instances under each head among

which individual preference is exercised. In the following series the classes are more general, and accordingly the scope for individual preference much larger: given a general term to name a particular instance under that term (537σ); given a picture to name some detail of it (447σ); given the word instead of the picture, to make a similar association (439σ); given the picture or the name to mention some property of it $(372\sigma$ and $337\sigma)$; given a quality to name an object to which it can be applied (351σ); given an intransitive verb to find an appropriate subject (527σ), or a transitive verb to find an appropriate object (379σ). Münsterberg has a series including a miscellaneous collection of such re-actions, and finds a time of 1036σ. Trautscholdt has investigated a similar series in which a specific instance of a general term had to be given, and finds a time of 1020σ (average of three subjects), 155σ of which must be deducted to get the pure association time.

Here, again, we may stop to consider a few generalizations which these results seem to sustain. The processes involved vary very considerably in the different experiments. Münsterberg cites as quick responses $(450\sigma-600\sigma)$ the instancing of ' a German wine (Rüdesheimer)," "of a number between ten and four (six),' "of a Greek poet (Homer);" as slow ones $(1200\sigma-1500\sigma)$, "a beast of the desert (lion)," "a French author (Voltaire)." Trautscholdt names " mast" as "a part of a ship" in 391σ, but requires 1899σ to name "art" as ' an æsthetic activity of man." These differences should appear in the average variations: that is, the average divergence of the re-action times from their mean. When the process is simple and constant, the average variation is small; when the processes are complicated and variable, the average variation is large. While in simple re-actions it is often less than 10 per cent of the re-action time, it is not infrequently as high as 30 per cent in the re-actions just considered. It may have been noticed that in certain cases the process in (2) was the reverse of that in (1). The one was a step from the whole to the part, the general to the special; while the other was from the part to the whole, the special to the general. In Cattell's case the former is the longer (433σ and 374σ). In Trautscholdt's results the conclusion comes out more clearly, the pure association time of an association of part to whole is 608σ; of whole to part, 901σ; of special to general, 754σ; of general to special, 947σ. It is thus easier to refer an individual object or quality to its class than to give an instance of a general concept. A similar result (namely, that the bond of association between two concepts is not equally strong in both directions) is derived from observing that it takes longer to recall that May precedes June than that June follows May, longer to go back and find a subject for a verb than to go forward and find an object for it, longer when given a quality to find an object possessing that quality than to recall a quality for an object, and so on.

We may here also conveniently consider the overlapping of mental processes, which we have found takes place whenever a series of simple processes, or a complex process involving many simple ones, is performed. The general truth that the time of a complex mental operation is less than the sum of the times needed for the performance of the separate factors into which the former may be resolved, will be again illustrated. Thus Münsterberg finds that it takes 103σ to name a specific instance of a class (e.g., to name a German river), 992σ to make a comparison, (e.g., Which is more important, — this river or that?) but only 1049σ to decide both questions together (e.g., Which is the most important German river?) In this case we clearly recognize that the last processes are not the sum of the preceding two, but that the category "most important German river" is already formed in the mind. The following comparisons are more illustrative. Instead of asking first, "Which is the most important German river?" (1049σ,) and then, "Which lies

more westerly, — Berlin, or the Rhine?" (992σ,) we ask
at once, "Which lies more westerly, — Berlin, or
the most important German river?" and find the time
1855σ, or 176σ less than the sum of the two foregoing
processes. Similarly, if instead of asking first, "On what
river is Cologne situated?" (848σ,) and then, "Which is
more westerly, — the Rhine or Berlin?" (992σ,) we ask at
once, "Which is more westerly, — Berlin, or the river on
which Cologne is situated?" we find a more remarkable
saving of time (1314σ, or 526σ less than the sum of the two
questions). This time was still further reduced to 1149σ
when the question was preceded by a list of a dozen cities.

(3) *Unlimited Associations.* When we pass to the re-
action of naming as rapidly as possible any word whatever,
that is suggested by a given word, we are drawing entirely
upon the natural associative habits of the individual, and
accordingly this method has been most useful in studying
psychological habits and tendencies. Our present purpose,
however, is only with the time-relations of this unrestricted
association. This has been the type of association first and
most frequently investigated, and it is customary to speak of
the "pure association time" as the total time minus the time
needed to repeat a word. Thus Münsterberg repeats a word
in 382σ, and calls out a word in association with the given
word in 896σ. Trautscholdt, however, who experimented
upon Wundt, Stanley Hall, and two other subjects, finds an
average time of 1024σ, 727σ of which is regarded as the
pure association time. Galton and others have made estimates, by rougher methods, of the rapidity with which
trains of ideas pass through the mind, and the result is a
rate not differing much in either direction from one association per second. It will be recognized at once that this process will be very different in different individuals and with
different words. Münsterberg's shortest association was
"gold–silver" (390σ); the longest, "sing–dance," "moun-

tain-level" (1100σ–1400σ). Trautscholdt also found "gold–silver" a very quick re-action (402σ), "storm–wind" (368σ), "duty–right" (415σ). Long re-actions were "God-fearing" (1132σ), "throne-king" (1437σ), "Karl–August" (1662ʊ). Some interesting inferences result from the consideration of the times of different types of these unrestricted associations Trautscholdt divides these into "word associations," or those suggested by the word rather than by the thing; "outer associations," or those relating to the sense-qualities of the object; and "inner" or logical associations. The results were 1033σ, 1028σ, 989σ, though this order may be liable to individual differences. Cattell and Berger have also compared the re-action times to concrete nouns (374σ, pure association time), to less concrete nouns (462σ), to abstract nouns (570σ), and to verbs (501σ), clearly showing that concrete terms are more readily suggestive than abstractions, and concrete objects more so than actions. Trautscholdt finds for associations to concrete nouns, 710σ; to actions, 837σ; to abstractions, 871σ.

Many of the influences to which we found simpler forms of re-action times open, are doubtless true of association times, but the great variability of the latter makes these difficult to establish. The effect of practice is noticed by Trautscholdt; and Cattell has shown that in students from thirteen to eighteen years of age a distinct shortening of the association time accompanies growth and education, while the students ranking higher in class have a somewhat shorter time than those standing low in class. Fatigue very readily enters, the accessible associations are easily exhausted, and the mind repeats itself very markedly. Changes under the action of drugs and in morbid mental states have been incidentally noticed, but still await systematic investigation.

The various processes, the times of which we have been studying, by no means exhaust the possibilities in this field. As our knowledge of mental operations becomes more perfect and more capable of experimental study, and as our power of analysis makes similar progress, the study of the time-relations of mental phenomena, already fertile in suggestions and results, will increase in interest and importance.

www.ingramcontent.com/pod-product-compliance
Lightning Source LLC
Chambersburg PA
CBHW021543270326
41930CB00008B/1346